Walks in Robin Hood's Yorkshire
Richard Bell

Contents

WILLOW
ISLAND
EDITIONS

In Robin Hood's Footsteps

Brockadale, Yorkshire, part of Barnsdale Forest

"My dwelling is in the wood." sayes Robin.
"By thee I set right nought:
My name is Robin Hood of Barnsdale.
A fellow thou hast long sought."

Robin Hood and Guy of Gisborne

ROBIN HOOD IS famous for this skirmishes with the Sheriff of Nottingham in Sherwood Forest but if you go back to the earliest ballads you find that the trail leads to Barnsdale Forest, 50 miles north of Nottingham.

How did Robin become an outlaw? Where did his rivalry with the Sheriff begin?

These six walks and two short town tours follow in the footsteps of a Yorkshire Robin Hood . . . and, more surprisingly, a Yorkshire Sheriff of Nottingham!

Access

For the most part these walks follow public and permissive rights of way or cross public parks and open spaces but diversion orders can be made and permissions withdrawn. We cannot of course be held responsible for such diversion orders and any inaccuracies in the text which result from these or other changes to routes nor any damage which might result from walkers trespassing on private property. We'd be grateful if you would e-mail us about any changes to routes at: **richard@willowisland.co.uk**

Most of these walks can be muddy in places and in **Brockadale** in particular the narrow path on the slope by the river *can be dangerous*.

Maps: OS Explorer 289 Leeds, 278 Sheffield & Barnsley, 288 Bradford & Huddersfield, 299 Ripon & Boroughbridge.

Waterways and rivers: several of the routes go close to open water. Always take special care of children when visiting waterways and towing paths, particularly near locks

Gramercy

(as they say 'thank you kindly' in the ballads) to the **countryside services** and **footpaths officers** of all the Yorkshire local authorities featured in these walks & to the **Yorkshire Wildlife Trust** at Brockadale. Also to **Richard Knowles** of Rickaro Books for tracking down some rare titles and to all the authors mentioned in my footnotes, especially **John Goodchild**, Wakefield archivist, and **Professor Helen Phillips** of the School of English Communication and Philosophy at Cardiff University who kindly agreed to check my manuscript. However, she warns me, the search for a 'real' 'historical' Robin Hood is fun . . . but nonsense! He is, after all, a *legend!*

ISBN 978-1-902467-19-1 © Richard Bell 2010, www.willowisland.co.uk
41 Water Lane, Middlestown, Wakefield, West Yorkshire, WF4 4PX

Robin . . . & Henry

NOTE: All events and characters in these comic strips come from historical records or the Robin Hood ballads

'Robin' is short for **Robert**. There were two **Robert Hodes** in the **Wakefield** area, one lived out at **Newton Hill**.

But there was only one **Henry de Faucumberg**!

In 1316 our Robin (Robert Hode of Wakefield) bought land on Bichil (probably *beech* hill because of the trees there rather than '*bitch*' hill').

From a map by John Goodchild, 1991

Robin and his wife **Matilda** paid 2 shillings (10 pence) to take a plot 30 x 16 feet from the 'lord's waste'.

They paid 6 pence a year rent to the lord of the manor and built a house of 5 rooms.

One of the neighbouring booths belonged to **Thomas Alayn** *(see page 29)*.

In the following year **Robert Hode** of Newton paid 6s. 8d. for leave to dig coal on **Alverthorpe Common**.

On 12th March 1313 **Faucumberg** had been fined for stealing wood from the lord of the manor's barn.

He was fined again for theft 3 times in the next 2 years!

Then in 1314 he was fined 12 pence for refusing to take the oath in the **Burgess Court**.

The Burgesses' Court was the town court; they would claim town cases from the **lord of the manor's Court**.

I hereby challenge this court!

The Knights Hospitallers of St. John of Jerusalem from Newland, Normanton, claimed immunity from the lord's fines.

(Both Robin & the Knights had property in Warrengate, Wakefield)

1285: Thornes farmer **Richard de Heya** argued that he could take the lord's deer!

I intend to take, whenever I can, all deer in my close, because that is my common chase!

Sources: Frame 1. *Robin Hood of Wakefield*, Harold Speak & Jean Forrester, p.3. 3. *Aspects of Medieval Wakefield and its Legacy*, John Goodchild, p.33. 4. *The True Story of Robin Hood*, J.W.Walker, p.7. 6. *Robin Hood, The Man Behind the Myth*, Graham Phillips & Martin Keatman, p.85. 5, 7, 8, 9, 10 *Wakefield its History & People*, J. W. Walker, pp. 105, 89, 89, 134 (double cross 135), 103.

Merry Wakefield

Why was the town known as 'Merry Wakefield' in medieval times?

On the feast of **Corpus Christi** in early summer, a cycle of **Mystery Plays** (Bible stories) was performed in the streets.

In the Wakefield version of the Nativity the shepherds have trouble with sheep rustlers near Horbury!

I have sought with my dogs All Horbury Shrogs. And of fifteen hogs Found I but one ewe

Local characters **Mak** and his wife **Gill** attempt to hide a lamb in a crib!

He was witched by an elf!

There's tax evasion too, when **Cain** cheats with his tithe to the church.

Cain, you offer wrong and of the worst.

He becomes the first outlaw after murdering his brother **Abel**. Cursed by God, he taunts his fellow men to catch and kill him.

And harshly when I am dead. Bury me at Goodybower at the quarry head.

At **Goodybower** – 'God i' the Bower' (now Trinity Walk) – stone was quarried for the rebuilding of the parish church (now the Cathedral).

In 1315 the central tower had collapsed.

The church was dedicated to **All Saints** and each one of them had a saint's day so the town enjoyed a lot of public holidays – literally 'holy days'.

The saint's statue was paraded to the quarry and displayed in a bower.

'Merry' Wakefield might refer to the worship of **Mary** – connected with the popular **Marian cult**, introduced by crusaders, palmers and troubadours – which flourished in the town.

The chantry chapel on the bridge (c. 1342) was dedicated to **the Virgin Mary**, the chapel on Westgate to **Mary Magdalene**

1339: **Margery**, wife of **John Pynder** owed the church 2s. 7d. for the assistance of **the girdle of the Blessed Mary**, which was supposed to assist women in childbirth.

Scenes of the life of the Virgin carved on the original chapel were acted out in the Mystery Plays – although several scenes were cut during the reformation.

The Virgin Mary was Robin's favourite saint and he later dedicated a chapel to Mary Magdalene in Barnsdale. Was he also connected with the Westgate chapel?

1-5, 11. *The Wakefield Mystery Plays (1961)*, Ed. Martial Rose, original text can be found online. **6, 7, 10.** *Wakefield its History & People*, J. W. Walker, pp. 177,178, 182 **8.** *The History & Topography of the Parish of Wakefield (1862)* John Hewit, p.13 **9.** *The White Goddess (1961)* Robert Graves, p. 396, *The Chantry Chapel of St. Mary on-the-Bridge(1972)*, Harold Speak & Jean Forrester, p.3.

The Pinder of Wakefield

George-a-Green; the Pinder's job was to round up stray animals from the open fields around the town. The lord of the manor's pinfold was on the Springs, next to the Waver, the town's water supply.

YOU CAN see some faces from Robin Hood's day if you're able to visit the **Chantry Chapel of St Mary on-the-Bridge** on one of its occasional open days. I guessed these were medieval carvings *(right)* but it seems that in his restoration of 1847 **George Gilbert Scott** *(1811-1878)* used a soft sandstone, which soon weathered in the then smoky atmosphere of Wakefield, so they're probably Victorian but they just look a lot older. The chapel as we see it today is mainly 20th century restoration but below pavement level the bridge and the pier the chapel stands on date from around 1342.

For hundreds of years, townsfolk pointed out the field where **George-a-Green**, 'The Jolly Pinder of Wakefield' fought **Robin Hood**, **Little John** and **Will Scarlet**, armed with with quarterstaff and buckler (a small round shield). This walk takes you past what became known as the Pinderfield.You'll get an impression as to why the outlaws should have chosen this quieter route into town, perhaps after crossing the Calder by boat at Kirkthorpe or Stanley Ferry.

Sculpture by Harry Malkin (point 3 on the walk).

*Calder valley seen from close to the site of the **Chantry Chapel of St Swithins** (at point 7, just before you turn onto this downhill path). This chapel, dating from c.1280 was provided for those suffering from the plague.*

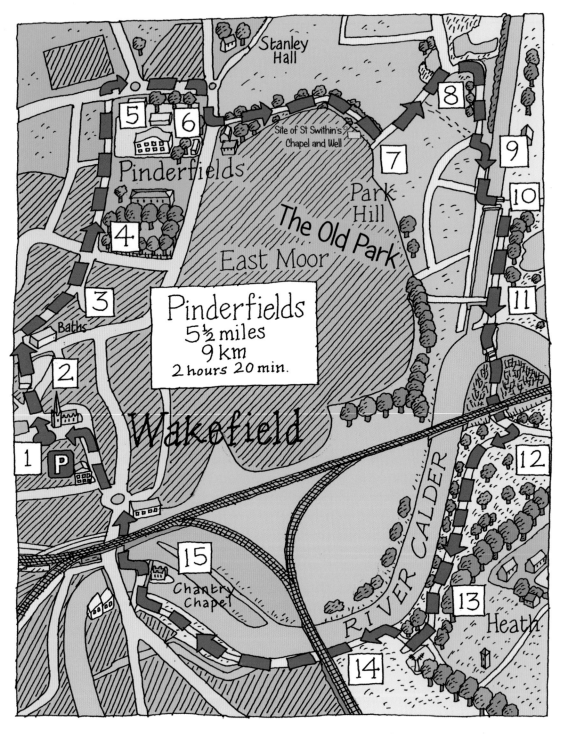

Stanley Hall

5 — 6

Site of St Swithin's Chapel and Well

8

7

9

10

Pinderfields

Park Hill

4

The Old Park

East Moor

3

11

Baths

Pinderfields
5½ miles
9 km
2 hours 20 min.

2

Wakefield

1

P

12

RIVER CALDER

15

Chantry Chapel

13

Heath

14

Parking: *town centre car parks.* **Buses:** *any Wakefield service* **OS ref.:** *SE 333208*

1. From the **Cathedral** tower head for the **bus station**, crossing the **Bull Ring** to **Union Street** in the far right corner to continue with the **Market Hall** on your left.

2. Go through the bus station building to the far end then cross at the crossing and turn right behind the **Lightwaves Leisure Centre** to walk along **York Street**.

3. When you arrive at the statue of the **Pinder of Wakefield** continue ahead (slightly to the left) along **Pinderfields Road**.

4. Cross **Eastmoor Road** and take the **Long Causeway** ahead.

5. In half a mile turn right on **Bar Lane**.

6. When you reach the second roundabout turn right back towards Wakefield for 50 yards on the **A642 Aberford Road** then cross at the crossing and take the footpath ahead, to the left of the barn conversion.

7. After half a mile bear left with the footpath down the slope across the fields towards **Stanley Flash nature reserve**.

8. When you reach the track at the bottom of the slope turn right, crossing a low railway sleeper bridge and continue on the track for a quarter of a mile, bearing right with the track when you reach the pylon wires.

9. At a T-junction with a track, turn left then right for 500 yards along the **Trans Pennine Trail south**.

10. At the next junction with a track, turn left to cross the canal, then turn immediately right along the **Trans Pennine Trail**.

11. In a third of a mile, ignoring a stone bridge over the canal on your right and the **Southern Washlands trail** on your left, cross the **River Calder** via the raised gantry bridge.

12. After passing through an osier bed and through an arch under the railway, continue on the track to the top of the banking and turn right on a path that runs along the embankment. This takes you alongside the river, largely hidden by bushes down to your right, for half a mile, with a scrubby area to your left, once occupied by the fly-ash lagoons of **Wakefield Power Station**.

13. After entering woodland, the path comes out on a concrete road with **Wakefield B electricity substation** on your left, which is all that now remains of the Power Station. In 100 yards when you cross a brook, turn immediately right on a path which takes you to the riverbank.

14. Follow the riverside path for a third of a mile then, as you reach **Fall Ings lock**, take the footbridge ahead across the canal to continue on the riverside path.

15. Cross the stone packhorse bridge and turn right to cross the **Chantry Chapel bridge**, then continue towards the main road to go under the railway bridge, passing the **Grey Horse** on your right. Make your way back into town via a concrete underpass. Cross **Kirkgate** to return to the **Cathedral**.

Poachers & Foresters

22nd November, 1274: in the manor court, **William the parker** is charged with taking **partridges, herons** and **deer** from the **Old Park** and of feathering his arrows with two grey-goose feathers and one white one, bound with white thread.

Brother Silvester, preceptor of the Knights of St John at Newland, is involved in the case.

> I refused the deer hide he had promised me!

There were **deer parks** to the north, south, east and west of **Wakefield**.

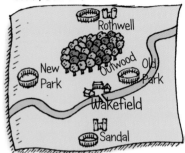

1297: Adam Hood – who we guess was Robin's father – was a **forester**, charged with protecting the lord's deer.

Like Robin's outlaws, he wore green in summer, grey in winter.

There were probably deer in **the Outwood** too, grazing at the clearing which gave **Lawns village** its name.

Robin had built his house near **Butchers' Row** on Wakefield market. An old tradition has it that Robin was a **butcher** . .

He met with poacher friends at a roadside well (at present-day **Robin Hood** village, but now lost) before going on to hunt at **Rothwell Park**.

Robin Hood's Hill lay on the southern edge of the Outwood. **Robin Hood's Close** at Outwood is mentioned in the manor court rolls in 1650.

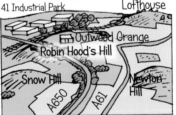

Robin Hood's Wind, a thaw wind, was said to be the only cold that the outlaw couldn't tolerate.

25th January, 1316: Robin's maidservant was fined 2d. for taking dry wood and vert (green vegetation) from the **Old Park**.

Deer killed in the **New Park** were gutted at **Humble Jumble Bridge**. Umbles means offal, especially of deer. They were used in 'Humble Pie'. **Jumble** referred to a heap of stones (or possibly to a bushy area). **Humble Jumble Beck**, now Bushy Beck, flowed via Alverthorpe into Westgate Beck - passing the chapel of Mary Magdalene.

Robin had a new house, a wife, a business, even a maidservant, and plenty of deer poaching opportunities. What could possibly go wrong?!

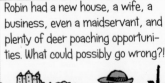

Frame 1.,2. *Wakefield its History & People*, J. W. Walker, p. 101 **4., 10.** *The True Story of Robin Hood (1952)*, J. W. Walker, p.2, 4, 26. **7.** *The Outlaw Robin Hood, His Yorkshire Legend*, Barbara Green p. 34. **9.** *Brewer's Dictionary of Phrase & Fable*, 15th edition **11.** *Shorter Oxford English Dictionary* (Walker in *Wakefield its History & People* suggests 'Humble' is from the Norse *humul*, a stone).

The Outwood

At **Lofthouse Nature Park**, on the former site of **Lofthouse Colliery**, **heather** has been planted on part of the restored spoil heap near **Lingwell Gate**. This is appropriate as Lingwell was the only place in the parish of Lofthouse where heather - also known as **ling** - grew.

IN ROBIN HOOD'S DAY, **wolf** and **wild boar** still roamed in the local forest. Tradition has it that **John of Gaunt** *(see my 'Walks in the Rhubarb Triangle')* killed the last wild boar at **Stye Bank** near Rothwell in 1380 and that 20 years later, at nearby **John of Gaunt's Hill**, the last wolf in Yorkshire was killed.

Even in Elizabethan times Wakefield's **Outwood** was so thick and extensive that a guide was employed to show travellers through.

Today an arm of the new **Forest of Leeds** almost connects with **Lofthouse Nature Park**, where thousands of trees are transforming the former colliery spoil heap into a wood that Robin and his father **Adam the forester** might recognise as a patch of the original Outwood.

You'll notice that there are a lot of 'gates' around the Outwood - Lofthouse Gate, Lingwell Gate, Carr Gate and Kirkhamgate for example. These gates prevented animals grazing on the common lands from straying into the villages*.

Vines, in a carving from the Cathedral, were grown in Wakefield in the warm climate of the middle ages but poor summers in the 1300s signalled the start of a 'Little Ice Age'.

Pigs and Acorns

In 1313 Robin was fined 4d for taking vert and **acorns**. **Pannage** was the right to allow pigs to feed on fallen acorns in a wood. The lord of the manor had awarded the right of pannage in the Outwood to the townsfolk (burgesses) of Wakefield prior to 1304.

If, as the Rothwell tradition suggests, Robin was a butcher, he may have needed supplies of vert (green vegetation) and acorns to fatten up any stock he had reared or bought at the market. On the same day that Robin and Matilda bought their plot on Bichill they paid the lord of the manor a shilling for a small piece of ground in Warrengate - perhaps for use as a stockyard.

If he was a poacher he might even have trained a pig as a retriever - pigs were smaller and sleeker than today's with dark, hairy skin like a wild boar - and, unlike a dog, he could sell the pork afterwards!

* The 'gate' in Westgate, Warrengate and Kirkgate is from the Viking 'gata' for a road or path.

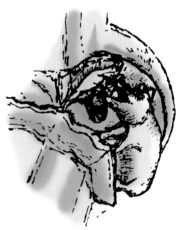

Pig eating acorns; *a medieval carving in* **Wakefield Cathedral.**

Robin Hood's Bridge, *lies 200 yards north of the summit of* **Robin Hood's Hill** *which rises to 87 metres (285 feet) where the A650 crosses the Leeds to London railway.*

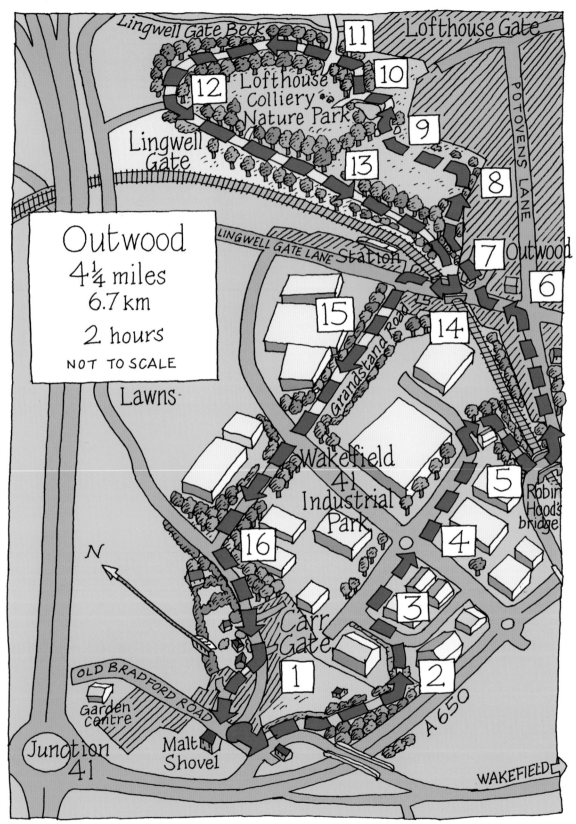

Parking: on the old **Bradford Road**, near **The Malt Shovel**, **Carr Gate**.

1. With the **Malt Shovel** on your right, walk back towards the end of the road. Turn left up **Bradford Road** and, just before the bridge over the **A650** dual carriageway, turn left on a public footpath on a tarmacked lane.

2. At the end of the lane the footpath continues between hawthorn hedges then alongside a warehouse.

3. When the footpath comes out on **Brunel Road**, turn left then right at the T junction.

4. At the roundabout go straight across down **Stephenson Way** opposite then in 300 yards, after a left-hand bend, take the footpath on your right then turn right again round the back of the building.

5. Turn left when you come out on **Potovens Lane**, crossing **Robin Hood's Bridge** and passing **Outwood Grange Academy** on your right. Continue for a quarter of a mile, passing **Outwood Park Medical Centre**.

6. At the crossroads turn left in the direction of **Outwood Station** and **Thorpe**.

7. Cross the road and, immediately after the bus stop, take the footpath that leads off **Lingwell Gate Drive**. You soon cross a cul-de-sac and then a stile and a bridge over a stream before emerging via railway sleeper steps at a playing field.

8. Turn right to make your way around the playing fields to the diagonally opposite right-hand corner.

9. Leave the field at the right-hand corner where a kissing gate takes you through to a triangular **duck pond**. Keep to the broad track around the pond area, leaving via a second kissing gate.

10. Take the public bridleway ahead, **'To Langley ½ mile'**, a broad path which takes you around the perimeter of the park.

11. At a crossroads of footpaths, ignore the turn to **'Langley ¼ mile'** on your right and continue on the **'Bradford Road, Carr Gate'** cycleway and footpath ahead.

12. At the top end, as the cycleway turns to the right, turn left over a stile by a gate and, ignoring a smaller path over a railway sleeper bridge to your left, continue ahead on the path on your right.

13. Continue on this path with the railway on your right. Don't turn back onto the playing fields but take the path by the railway on your right.

14. At the small parking area near **Outwood Station**, walk up the concrete steps and turn right over the bridge.

15. Immediately after passing **Lingwell Court** on your right, turn left on **Grandstand Road** and follow this straight ahead for half a mile, crossing a service road of the industrial estate.

16. Turn left at the T junction with **Lawns Lane** then in a quarter of a mile after passing **Lawns Court**, take the footpath on your right opposite **Tudor Lawns**. This takes you behind houses to come out on a small road which emerges opposite the **Malt Shovel**.

The Fishlake Church

FOR OVER TWO CENTURIES the **Earls de Warenne** had been **lords of the manor** of Wakefield but that was all about to change with disastrous consequences for Robert Hode and his wife Matilda. In this walk we follow the old London road into Wakefield – now a quiet track called **Milnthorpe Lane**. You'll see how the castle dominated the approach to the town. As well as a deer park, the castle had a farm, a forest, two mills (one at Newmillerdam) and two fishponds, although fish always died in the smaller pond near the castle. Sandal also had a **Fishlake Church** . . .

In 1078 the Warennes had given the **Fishlake Church** to French Cluniac monks of **Lewes Priory, Sussex.**

14th August, 1294, **John** and **William de Warenne** were given **dispensations** by the **Bishop of Hereford** (his successor was a famous rival of Robin in the ballads) so that despite being illegitimate sons of the Earl they could start a career in the church.

Willaim rose to become a prior while **John** became **Rector of the Fishlake Church** but in March 1313 he is charged with misconduct with **Matilda Malbuche.**

And with Alice Benet!

The **Archbishop of York** pardons him – on condition that he pays £20 towards the fabric of **York Minster**.

John's half-brother was **John de Warenne**, the **8th Earl** *(1285-1347)* and **lord of the manor of Wakefield.**

The Earl sometimes wore a horned helmet!

He was attempting to divorce his young wife **Joan of Bar** in order to marry **Maude de Nerford**.

In 1327, with trouble brewing between France and England, the **king** went to court and won control of the Fishlake Church from the French Cluniac monks.

He argued with **Pope John XXII** (based in Avignon, not Rome)over who should be Rector of Fishlake.

Geffery de Cotes!

Peter Vanrelli!

1317: More trouble for **John, Earl de Warenne**: one of his squires kidnaps **Alice de Lacy** the Earl of Lancaster's wife!

Thomas, Earl of Lancaster is the most powerful baron in England. He lays siege to Sandal Castle.

Archaeologists found traces of destruction in the bailey

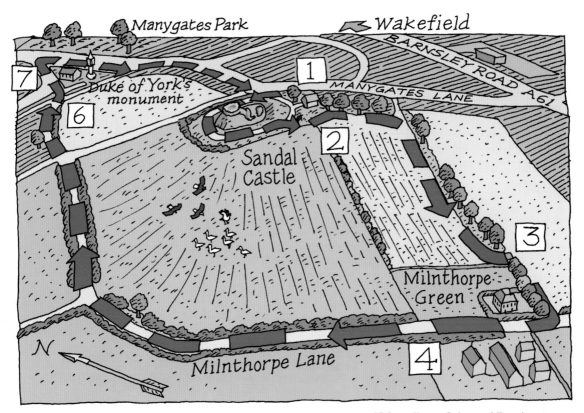

Sandal Castle

1¾ miles, 3 km, 45 minutes
OS ref. SE 339 181 **Buses**: 59, 110, 194, 195, 196

1. Facing the castle, turn right from the car park to make an anti-clockwise tour of the path around the moat.

2. Three-quarter's of the way around, before you reach the visitor centre, look for a path near a bench down the rough slope into the right-hand corner of the castle grounds. Go through the stile and continue along the top edge of the field. When you reach the corner, turn right with the path down the slope, following the hedgerow on your left.

3. A timber bridge at the bottom corner takes you through into the next field. Turn right, then when you reach **Milnthorpe Lane,** right again.

4. Follow the lane – which becomes a track, then a footpath fringed by hedges – for half a mile, ignoring a footpath to the left.

5. At a crossroads with a footpath (back to the castle up the slope to your right or down to **Pugneys Country Park** on your left) continue ahead on the tarmacked

footpath with flats to your left.

6. When you arrive at a skewed crossroads of tarmacked paths take the second path on your left down the slope to **Milnthorpe Lane**. Go straight down the lane towards **Manygates Park**.

7. Turn right on **Manygates Lane**, passing the **Education Centre** and the **Duke of York's memorial** on your right as you return up the slope to the castle.

13

King Edward and his Merry Men

The king, Edward II was unlike his warlike father, Edward I. He preferred the company of merry men.

He paid **Jak de St Albon**, the Painter Royal, 50 shillings for 'dancing on the table before the king which made him laugh beyond measure'.

He preferred thatching, digging ditches and shoeing horses to jousting and hunting.

In 1315–16 he toured the Fens with a 'silly company of swimmers'.

His favourite merry man was **Piers Gaveston**. In 1308, when the king went to France for his marriage, he appointed Gaveston as regent, enraging the Earl of Lancaster and the barons.

His new Queen, **Isabella**, was also known as 'The She-Wolf of France'. This wasn't going to work out well for Edward!

1312: Lancaster raises an army and pursues the king and Gaveston from York to Newcastle.

Newcastle   Tynemouth

The king and Gaveston escape by sea. Leaving Gaveston at **Scarborough Castle**, the king returns to York to gather support.

The barons – including **John Earl de Warenne** – lay siege to the castle. Gaveston gives himself up on condition he gets a fair trial.

But on July 1st 1312 Lancaster and the barons have him beheaded.

Vowing revenge at first, the king later pardons the barons. In 1317, after the kidnap of **Alice de Lacey** he settles the feud between the two Earls by taking Sandal Castle and the manor of Wakefield from Warenne and giving them to Lancaster.

Robin and Matilda now have a new lord of the manor but John, the Earl of Warenne wouldn't have to wait long for his revenge on Lancaster.

Sources include: *The Cult of 'St' Thomas of Lancaster and its Iconography, Yorkshire Archaeological Journal, Vol. 64, 1992*

The Battle of Boroughbridge

In **November 1316** Robin was fined for not enlisting in the king's army to fight Scottish raiders but – as he *wasn't* fined in the call-up in the following year – it seems that he joined the king's army in the unsuccessful attack on **Berwick-on-Tweed**. In 1320 the king returned to lay siege to Berwick but the Scots led a counter attack, defeating a makeshift force led by the Archbishop of York at the **Battle of Myton** (2 miles east of Boroughbridge) before pillaging Yorkshire, crossing the Aire at Castleford bridge.

There was another call to arms in 1322 but this time it was the new lord of the manor of Wakefield, the **Earl of Lancaster**, who needed 1,000 archers to fight in open rebellion against the king.

Lancaster's archers wore **Lincoln green** livery.

Wednesday 10th March: meeting the king's army at **Burton-on-Trent**, Lancaster realises he is outnumbered. He burns the town before heading back north.

Safe in his castle at **Pontefract**, the barons, including Roger Clifford, lord of Skipton, persuade Lancaster to go north to his castle at Dunstanburgh.

Heading up the Great North Road, the rebels stop at **Boroughbridge** but, marching overnight from Ripon, **Sir Andrew Harcla**, under orders from the king, takes control of the bridge.

Tuesday 16th March: Harcla's archers hold back Lancaster's knights.

From underneath the bridge a Welsh soldier in Harcla's force spears the rebel **Earl of Hereford** through a chink in the planks.

Lancaster attempts to cross the nearby ford but archers and a shield formation of spearmen prevent his knights crossing the river.

It's possible that Harcla – an old comrade of Lancaster's – might have agreed terms of surrender but that night **Henry de Faucumberg** arrives. He is taking a break from his post as **Sheriff of Nottingham** *(see p.24)* to take command of the king's 'Yorkshire Array'.

Lancaster's men start to drift away overnight. He is arrested next morning as he prays in the chapel (point 4 on the walk).

Forced to wear the livery of one of his servants, Lancaster is taken by boat down the river to York. The other barons are made to walk, apart from Clifford who, because he has a head wound, also travels in the boat.

Lancaster in the boat, 1322, York Minster had only a central tower.

Sources: *Battles Fought in Yorkshire (1891)*, Alex. D. H. Leadman, *The Battles and Battle Fields of Yorkshire (1854)*, William Grange, **Faucomberg:** *List of the High Sheriffs of York;* http://midgleywebpages.com/yorksheriffs.html also http://www.channel4.com/history/microsites/H/history/n-s/robin03.html#sheriff **Boat:** pilgrim badge, Pontefract, *Brit.Mus.*

Boroughbridge

ON THIS WALK we first cross the river to visit the positions defended by **Harcla's** archers and spearmen, holding the bridge on behalf of the king. There was no canal at that time but it's believed that the ford, where Lancaster (and therefore our Robin Hood) fought, was approximately where Milby lock is today. We return to the southern bank of river to see the battlefield from Lancaster's point of view. Under enemy fire and with a formation of spearmen holding opposite bank, the river proved an impassable barrier.

*Medieval **monument** to Harcla's victory at the Battle of Boroughbridge. This originally stood in the town's market place but it was removed on 21st April, 1852, and re-erected in Aldborough. The **fountain** (left), fed by an artesian well, was built in St. James Square, Boroughbridge in 1875.*

Continuing on the riverside path you can imagine the jeering victors following the boat on which the captive, humiliated, Lancaster was sent downstream to York.

*Deer hoof-prints in a Roman tile **tegula** found in Isurium. The tile had probably been laid out to dry before firing.*

On the return journey there's a chance to go much further back in time to see the Roman mosaics of **Isurium** (Alborough).

The English Heritage **Aldborough Roman Site** is open weekends and bank holidays, 1 Apr-30 Sep. Tel. 01423 322768

The Devil's Arrows

IN ROBIN HOOD'S time there may have been four **Devil's Arrows** at Boroughbridge. The fourth might have been broken up and used in the building of a small bridge nearby. Erected some 4,000 years ago the arrows are millstone grit monoliths from **Plumpton Rocks** (SE 357536), three miles south of Knaresborough and nine miles south-west of Boroughbridge.

Plumpton Rocks might have made a good hide-out for Robin and his companions as they fled south after the battle.
OS ref. SE 391664, Roecliffe Lane, Boroughbridge.

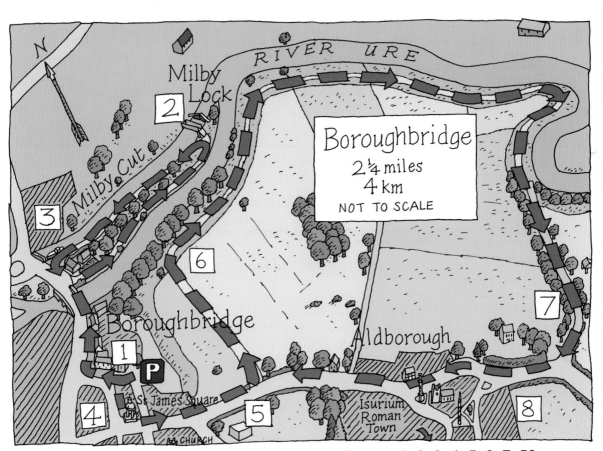

1¾ hours

Parking: Back Lane car park off High Street.

Buses: 1, 2, 3, 4, 5, 6, 7, 56, 56A, 57, 57A, 812,

1. From the car park cross **Hall Square** then turn right on **Fishergate** and right again to cross the bridge over the **River Ure**. At the end of the bridge take the riverside footpath on your right.

2. Follow the riverside path to **Milby Lock** then return to the town using the right-hand path alongside the canal.

3. After passing the moorings, take the steps to your left by the concrete road bridge, to get back to the road. Return across the river to the town centre.

4. Passing Hall Square on your left, continue along **High Street** to **St James Square** (*site of the chapel until 1851*) then turn left to leave the square heading in the direction of Aldborough.

5. Bear left on the **Aldborough Road** out of town and take the first footpath on your left across the fields.

6. Turn right with the path up onto the flood bank and continue for a mile, passing through three metal kissing gates.

7. At the end of the flood bank, the path comes out on a tarmacked lane. Follow this away from the river and when you reach the road turn right into the village of **Aldborough**.

8. Passing the church and monument on your left, return via the road to Boroughbridge.

17

Escape to the Greenwood

March 1322: Lancaster's rebels are declared outlaws.

One story has Robin escaping to **Scarborough** in times of trouble. He lodges with an old woman who offers him work on a fishing boat (salted herring was often on the menu at Sandal Castle).

He wishes he was hunting fallow deer 'in **Plumpton Park**'.

But Robin saves the day when the fishermen are attacked by a French ship.

England's greatest enemies at the time were France and Scotland, which might explain why the French were sailing off Scarborough.

He might be thinking of **Plumpton Park** near Knaresborough – a place to which a band of archers might have escaped after the Battle of Boroughbridge *(see page 16)*.

Declared **outlaws** after the battle, with their bows, arrows and Lincoln green livery Robin and his fellow archers were well equipped to spend the coming spring and summer living rough. If Robin had been a **butcher** (which he claims is his craft in *Robin Hood and the Butcher*) and a ***poacher*** he was well trained to survive in the greenwood.

Brockadale lay at the northern edge of **Barnsdale Forest**. It is marked as **Broken Dale** on old maps because of limestone quarrying.

With its river and craggy rocks and the iron age earthworks of **Castle Hill** on top, Brockadale offered a defendable position for a band of archers.

In one of the ballads, Robin boasts to the Sheriff that he has a castle and towers – did he mean Castle Hill and the surrounding tower-like crags?

Wentbridge is mentioned in the ballad as the place where Robin meets, and fights, a **Potter**.

Sayles, now Sayles Plantation, is mentioned in several ballads. On this walk you'll see what a good look-out post it would have made *(see page 26)*. The ballads refer to **Watling Street**, which is what this section of the **Great North Road** was called. The A1 flyover, built in 1961, is 30 metres (100 ft) high.

Barnsdale Forest was notorious for its outlaws for centuries and important travellers were given extra guards for this part of their journey. It would have been easy for the outlaws to melt away into neighbouring Sherwood to the south but it would also have been possible to make undercover visits to the nearest town, **Pontefract**, only 5 miles away.

A recently discovered (in 1993) version *Robin Hood and the Butcher* is included in *Robin Hood, The Forresters Manuscript (1998)*, edited by Stephen Knight

Life in the Greenwood

I'VE KNOWN Brockadale for years without realising that it had a Robin Hood connection. On one occasion I was leading a walking group along the muddy path beside the **River Went** when one of my walkers, a 75 year old woman, fell in. On another occasion a friend slipped down the banking and had to

be rescued by air ambulance. *Please take great care on this walk!*

Amongst the flowers growing on the magnesian limestone in the **Yorkshire Wildlife Trust's** Brockadale nature reserve is

Perforate St John's Wort which the Knights of St John used to treat wounds. According to the doctrine of signatures, those little perforations which you can see when you hold a leaf to the light are a clue to its medicinal qualities.

Yew was used for bows, **Ash** for arrows and a glue was made from **Bluebell** bulbs for fixing the arrowhead to the shaft.

You're as likely to see (or hear the laughing 'yaffle' call of) the **green woodpecker** in Brockadale's wild flower meadows as you are to see it in the woods.

Yorkshire Wildlife Trust:
www.ywt.org.uk

Hartstongue and Herb Robert (robert = red, as in robin) grow by the outcrops of magnesian limestone.

Perforate St John's Wort

juvenile & an adult.
Green Woodpeckers

Woodlouse; was called Robin Hood's Steed because it ran out from the Yule log (see page 28)

Robin Hood plaque on the bridge at Wentbridge

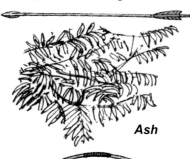

Ash

Yew in hedge, Wentbridge

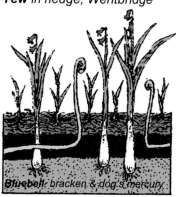

Bluebell, bracken & dog's mercury

19

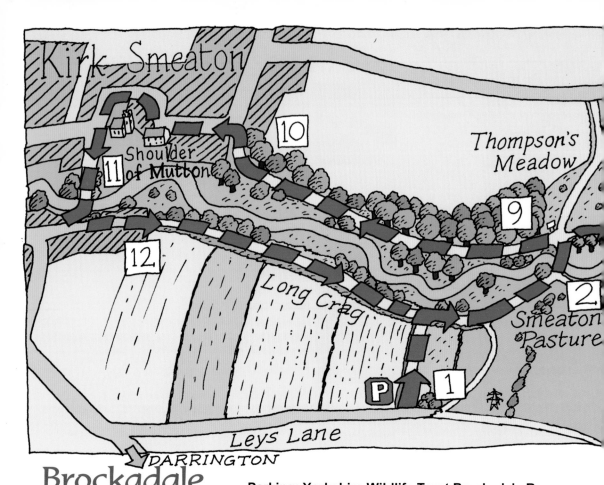

Brockadale

5¼ miles 8.4 km. 2½ hours
OS ref. SE 513 173

Parking: Yorkshire Wildlife Trust Brockadale Reserve
car park, **Ley Lane**, your first left turn as you leave **Kirk
Smeaton** on **New Road** heading towards **Darrington**.

1. From the car park take the path to the **Yorkshire Wildlife Trust Brockadale Reserve**. Go through the kissing gate and turn right to follow the path along the valley side.

2. After walking down across **Smeaton Pasture** and entering a belt of trees, cross the footbridge over the **River Went**, bear left with the path then, when you arrive at **Thomp-son's Meadow**, turn right along the banking.

3. A kissing gate takes you into **Brockadale** woods. The path follows the course of an old mineral railway for the next half a mile.

4. Please take great care on this next section; it's not clear where the right of way goes but there doesn't seem to be any choice than to go down to a narrow path alongside the river when you first see it down a short slope to your right, immediately after a mossy boulder. In about 100 yards, after passing some small craggy outcrops of limestone, make your way back up the slope via the first reasonable path.

5. Walk under the A1 viaduct, ignoring a couple of footpaths to your left and continuing on the main path ahead towards **Wentbridge.**

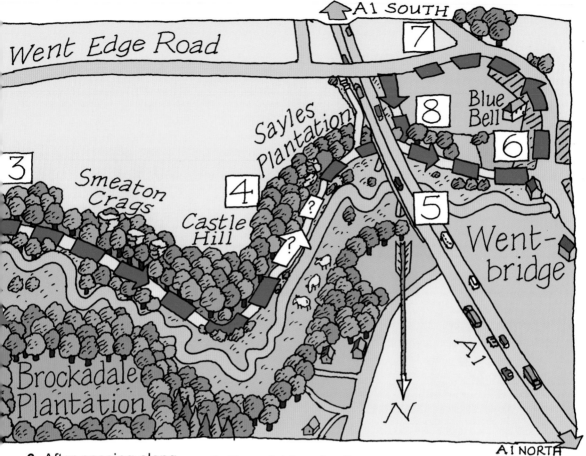

6. After passing along the right-hand edge of two fields you come out on the **Great North Road** in the village. Turn left *(or turn right to see the **Robin Hood plaque** on the **bridge**)* passing **The Bluebell** as you climb the hill.

7. As you near the top of the slope take the road on the left to '*Kirk Smeaton*' and '*A1 South*'. Just before you reach the bridge over the A1 turn left down the concrete steps then walk along the top of the roadside embankment before descending back into Brockadale.

8. Turn right under the viaduct and retrace your steps *(with care!)* to Thompson's Meadow.

9. Leave Thompson's Meadow via the kissing gate straight ahead to continue towards **Kirk Smeaton** with the river on your left. A number of kissing gates take you through woodland and riverside pastures then alongside a barbed wire fence on your left as you approach the village.

10. The footpath bears right up the slope via a sunken lane that brings you out on a bend in the village's **Main Street**.

Turn left and in 300 yards, when you pass a small park by the **church**, take the tarmacked path down towards the river.

11. Cross the footbridge, climb up **Hodge Lane** and in 100 yards turn left on **Chapel Lane**.

12. In 100 yards take the footpath ahead, immediately to the right of the converted chapel, and continue for half a mile through woodlands and along the top of **Long Crag** to return to the start of the walk.

21

A Saint in Pomfret

Sunday, 21st March 1322, five days after the battle, the king has Lancaster brought to **Pontefract**.

Monday: At a mock trial, **John Earl de Warenne** and the king's new favourite **Hugh le Despenser** (Elder) are amongst those sitting in judgement.

With an old friar's hood on his head Lancaster is set on a lean white horse without a bridle. He is taken to a hill to the north of the castle.

> King of Heaven have mercy on me, for the king of earth hath foresaken me.

The jeering crowds roll balls of soil to remind him that soon his head will roll on the ground.

> Sir traitor, turn thee towards the Scots* thy foul death to undergo.

*He had been accused of plotting with **Robert the Bruce**.

Hugh de Müston, 'a villain of London' makes a botched job of the execution, taking two or three blows to cut off his head.

Monks from Pontefract's Priory Church beg for his body from the king. They bury him on the right side of the high altar.

Now things start to change: there are miracles at the tomb – a blind priest regains his sight, a child drowned in a well is restored to life.

Baldock the chancellor orders 14 well armed French soldiers to watch the hill.

But Pontefract is soon a place of pilgrimage: Lancaster is seen as a martyr. A chapel is built on the hill. He's portrayed on pilgrims badges and in effigy in St Pauls, London.

24th August, 1323: **Archbishop Melton of York** complains of the danger of the huge crowds that are gathering – people have been killed in the demonstrations.

But bowing to public pressure, the **Queen**, the Archbishop and, eventually the **new king** ask the **Pope** to declare Lancaster a saint.

In 1359 it is recorded that 'blood ran out of the tomb of Lord Thomas, formerly Earl of Lancaster, at Pontefract.'

Sources: *The Cult of 'St' Thomas of Lancaster and its Iconography, Yorkshire Archaeological Journal, Vol. 64, (1992)* John Edwards, *Battles Fought in Yorkshire (1891)*, Alex. D. H. Leadman

Pontefract Castle

The castle is open daily 10.30 a.m. until dusk (8.30 a.m. to dusk, weekdays). Admission is free.

THE LANDSCAPED mound at the end of the inner bailey contains the un-excavated remains of the castle's **Great Hall**, where the trial of **Thomas of Lancaster** was held.

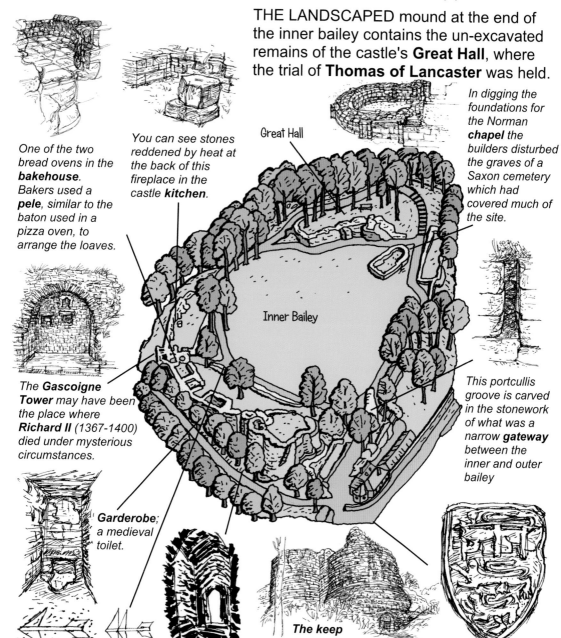

In digging the foundations for the Norman **chapel** the builders disturbed the graves of a Saxon cemetery which had covered much of the site.

One of the two bread ovens in the **bakehouse**. Bakers used a **pele**, similar to the baton used in a pizza oven, to arrange the loaves.

You can see stones reddened by heat at the back of this fireplace in the castle **kitchen**.

Great Hall

Inner Bailey

The **Gascoigne Tower** may have been the place where **Richard II** (1367-1400) died under mysterious circumstances.

This portcullis groove is carved in the stonework of what was a narrow **gateway** between the inner and outer bailey

Garderobe; a medieval toilet.

Carvings, probably mason's marks.

Grid iron pattern - a game?

Dungeon below the keep, is not open to the public, but there are organised visits to the **Magazine** (right) below the bailey.

The keep

The **arms of the House of Lancaster** are built into the wall of a house which stands opposite the modern entrance to the castle. The **barbican**, a strongly fortified gatehouse, once stood here.

23

Robin and the Sheriff

The first **Baron Henry de Faucumberg** was given the **Manor of Cuckney** in **Sherwood Forest** for shoeing King William's horse

January 1295: When **William de Faucumberg** dies, his son **Henry** takes control of Cuckney and of the family estate at **Catfoss** in **Holderness, East Yorkshire.**

Somehow Henry had prevented his older brother **John** from inheriting. It was alleged that John was mentally unfit to inherit. Was he the **Little John** of the Robin Hood ballads?

When Little John tricks his way into the Sheriff of Nottingham's household, he disguises himself as **Ranolf Greenleaf** of *Holderness* – where the Faucumberg family had their estate.

Despite his former set-backs *(see p. 3),* Henry de Faucumberg rose to become not only **Sheriff of Nottinghamshire** (1318-19 & 1323-25) but also **Sheriff of Yorkshire** (1325-27 & 1328-30).

In February 1324 he was given the job of seizing the property of Contrariants (rebels) in Derbyshire, Staffordshire and Shropshire.

As a reward he was given land in Yorkshire seized from one of the rebels.

Mine! all mine!

Robin's house on Bichil was forfeited. In 1357 it is described as 'formerly in the tenure of Robert Hode.'

At times the Sheriff was made keeper of Nottingham and of York Castle but the castles were never his property.

The Sheriff and his wife may have run an inn near the market place in Nottingham; Robin (in disguise) lodges with them in *Robin Hood and the Butcher.*

At the end of the ballad, returning from Robin Hood's camp, the Sheriff tells his wife asks how he has fared 'so far in the north country'

This suggests that the meeting took place in Barnsdale. 50 miles to the north, rather than in nearby Sherwood.

Source: *Robin Hood -The Man Behind the Myth (1995),* Graham Phillips & Martin Keatman, *p.85,* who quote *Robin Hood: An Historical Enquiry (1985),* John Bellamy. **Frame 1.** Ancient Ancestors website: http://members.pcug.org.au/~ronwells/260-9.htm

Barnsdale Forest

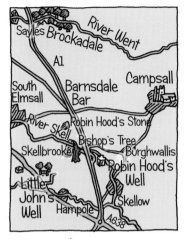

IN 1194 King Richard was hunting a stag in the eastern part of Sherwood Forest when it escaped into neighbouring Barnsdale. He ordered 'that no person should kill, hunt or chase the said hart, but that he might safely returne into forrest againe'. Medieval forests were so extensive that you could pass from one to the next without realising it.

Brockadale, only 4 miles from Pontefract was on the northern fringe of Barnsdale (with Sherwood further south). Heading south today on the A1 from Brockadale you pass the only point, 500 metres north of Barnsdale Bar, where the modern counties of West, East and South Yorkshire meet.

Robin Hood's Stone, about, 500 metres south of the Bar, was a landmark, now lost, which was mentioned in 1422 in a deed of **Monk Bretton Priory**. Monk Bretton Priory was dedicated to St Mary Magdelene, as is the church at **Campsall** *(left)*, where tradition has it that Robin and Marian were married. Robin told King Edward:

> *"I made a chapel in Bernysdale,*
> *That semely is to se.*
> *It is of Mary Magdalen,*
> *And thereto wolde I be."*

> *A Little Gest of Robin Hood*

Campsall Church (SE 545191).

The **Bishop's Tree** near Skelbrooke was pointed out as the one that Robin made the Bishop of Hereford dance a jig around in the ballad. Like the stone, it has since disappeared.

The canopy to Robin Hood's Well (SE 519118) designed by Sir John Vanbrugh (1664-1726). Heading south on the A1, as soon as you pass the turn to 'The Burghwallis',you need to start pulling in to the Manor Farm lay-by to see it. After damage in collision the monument was dismantled in 1960 and rebuilt a few hundred yards further south in 1964.

The **River Skell** is associated with **Little John**. He is said to have met and fought Robin on a narrow bridge across the river (actually a brook). Tradition suggests that *skell* is from 'skelp', a blow, clap or slap with the open hand.

Little John's Well (SE 545191), now damaged, at the roadside near a junction west of Hampole.

Walking? - unfortunately there are no footpaths to Robin Hood's Well!

Sources: *The Outlaw Robin Hood, His Yorkshire Legend*, 1991, Barbara Green, *Robin Hood of Wakefield*, 1970, Harold Speak & Jean Forrester, *The Haunts of Robin Hood*, 1970, W. R. Mitchell

The Sorrowful Knight

The first story in the famous **Little Gest of Robin Hood** is set entirely in Yorkshire.

"Robin stood in **Barnsdale**
And leaned him to a tree:
And by him stood **Little John**.
A good yeoman was he."

Robin sends Little John, **William Scarlok** (also known as Scarlet or Scathelock, 'Lock-breaker') and **Much** up to **Sayles** to look for a 'dinner guest' (one who will subsequently be asked to pay!).

They look east and west on **Watling Street** but there are no travellers in sight – which is perhaps not surprising as this stretch of the Great North Road is notorious for outlaws! So they look in **Barnsdale Forest**.

They meet with a ragged, **sorrowful knight** who is travelling by '**a dern strete**' (a hidden way) with his hood pulled over his eyes – he obviously wants to escape notice.

My master is Robin Hood

He is a good yeoman, of him have I heard much good.

The knight had been heading south:

My purpose was to have dined today in Blyth or Doncaster.

Robin's Camp

Little John takes the knight to Robin's '**lodge-door**'. A lodge is a temporary shelter used when hunting. The lodge could be a tent, a shed, or a **bower**: a living shelter formed from trees, interwoven with branches and climbing plants.

Forest Fayre

After washing & wiping their hands the feast includes:
Bread & wine
Umbles *(see p.8)* of the deer
Swans
Pheasants
Fowls of the River
& little birds that bred on briar

Robin learns that – through no fault of his own – the knight owes £400 to a rich Abbott.

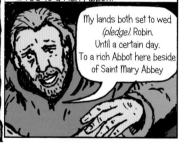

My lands both set to wed *(pledge)*, Robin. Until a certain day, To a rich Abbot here beside of Saint Mary Abbey

The Knight explains that he is fleeing the country on pilgrimage to Jerusalem because his former friends won't help him. Invoking Jesus and God or Peter, Paul and John fails to persuade Robin that he should help the knight but when the knight mentions '**Our dear Lady**' Robin sees him as '**Our Lady's Messenger**' and agrees to help.

Robin gives the knight a good horse, fresh colourful clothes, a new saddle, a pair of gilded spurs and £400 from his treasury.

With Little John acting as his squire the knight sets off to York and, to the consternation of the rich Abbot and his 'fat-headed' high cellarer, pays off his debt and wins back his estates.

York

IF YOU walk along the city walls behind the Minster, from Bootham Bar to Monk Bar, you come to **Robin Hood's Tower** at the corner. It has had this name since 1622; in Robin Hood's day it was known as the **Bawing Tower**. It was rebuilt in 1888-89 using concrete reinforced with tram rails in its structure.

Hobbehod was the nickname of the outlaw **Robert Hod** (possibly also known as Robert of Wetherby), who was hunted down and apparently hanged in York *c.* 1226.

Roger de Clifford, *Lord of Skipton, one of the rebel barons who fought at Boroughbridge, was hanged in chains from the walls of York Castle - now better known as* **Clifford's Tower**.

Part of the **north aisle and transept** *of the abbey church, c. 1290.*

St Mary's Abbey

St Olave's Church

Gatehouse & Lodge

The Yorkshire Museum: *remains of the abbey's chapter house and warming house can be seen in the basement of the museum.*

The Multangular Tower *dates from about 210 A.D. You can see Roman stonework at its base and in the adjoining stretch of the city wall.*

The ground floor of the **Hospitium** *dates from the 1300s but the upper storey is mainly a modern restoration. This was probably the place where lower status guests - such as Little John - would have been accommodated.*

Where the Hart is

*"Yonder I saw a right fair hart,
His colour is of green"*

Stag antler headdress,
Star Carr, North
Yorkshire, 7,500 B.C.

Says Little John as he tricks the Sheriff into a meeting with Robin in the forest. He describes the merry men as 'seven score of deer', each with sixty sharp tines on their antlers.

"Lo, here is the master hart." he says as they meet Robin, who forces the Sheriff to join him in a feast. Robin is famous for his feasts in the forest, dining on the king's deer, but his connection with merry making and revelry seems to go deeper than that.

Yorkshire has a long tradition of deer ritual; the 21 sets of antlers found at excavations of the Mesolithic lake village at **Star Carr** near Pickering are 9,500 years old, dating back almost to the last ice age. They had been modified for use as headdresses, possibly as a disguise when hunting but more likely for use in ritual. One of the reindeer antlers used in the annual **Horn Dance** at **Abbots Bromley**, Staffordshire, has been carbon dated to the time of the Norman conquest. Maid Marian and a boy Bowman appear in the Abbots Bromley dance.

'From time immemorial', wrote **John Hewitt** in 1862, at Christmas time the sword or rapier dancers of Wakefield performed the dramas of *Robin Hood* and the *Pinner of Wakefield*.

'Robin Hood became closely associated with the May Day revels,' wrote poet and mythologist **Robert Graves**, 'By his successful defiance of the ecclesiastics Robin became such a popular hero that he was later regarded as the founder of the Robin Hood religion, and its primitive forms are difficult to recover.'

He suggests a connection with **Yuletide** but also with the Marian cult, which was popular in Yorkshire. The first recorded use of the name Marion was in the Yorkshire Poll Tax Return of 1379. Robin's wife Matilda is said to have taken the outlaw name of Marian.

As Robin's fame grew, the nobility wanted to claim him as one of their own. Henry VIII played the part of Robin Hood in courtly revels. In later ballads Robin became the outlawed knight **Sir Robert of Loxley** and by the time **Charlotte Brontë** imagines the grave at 'Nunnely' (Kirklees Park) in her novel *Shirley*, he has become an Earl:

> *"the ghost of the Earl of Huntingdon . . . and the shadowy ring of his merry men under the canopy of the thickest, blackest, oldest oak in Nunnely Forest . . . a phantom abbess, or mist-pale nun, among the wet and weedy relics of that ruined sanctuary of theirs, mouldering in the core of the wood."*

Paragraph 1. *The Little Gest of Robin Hood.* **4.** *The History and Topography of the Parish of Wakefield (1862)* John Hewitt, *p.131.* **5.** *The White Goddess (1961)* Robert Graves, *p. 397.* **6.** *Robin Hood of Wakefield* Harold Speak & Jean Forrester, *p.3.* **8.** *Shirley (1849)*, Charlotte Brontë, *Chapter 29.*

Hartshead

Castle Hill, Almondbury, visible beyond Huddersfield on a clear day

Robin Hood's Grave

Castle Hill

Kirklees Hall, 1610, built with stone from Kirklees Priory

15th century **Priory Gatehouse** (not visible).

Park Wall

ON THIS last walk you'll get views across **Kirklees Park** but there is no public access to **Robin Hood's Grave** or to the **Priory Gatehouse** associated with the story of his death. I'm glad the grave *isn't* on the tourist trail; I'm sure Robin would rather be resting in peace in quiet, well-wooded parkland . . . with an occasional roe deer wandering by, of course!

Carvings on the porch of **The Three Nuns** *(point 3 on the walk).*

In 1536 when Kirklees Priory was closed during Henry VIII's dissolution of the monasteries, it's said that **Three Nuns** (shown here in a carving above the entrance to the pub), Cecilia Topcliffe, Joan Leverthorpe and Katherine Grice, started running the local inn.

*Not only do we have a **Hartshead** and a **Roehead** within a mile of Robin Hood's grave but there's also a curious reference in Robin Hood's day to one of the nuns at Kirklees Priory being censured for wearing a 'horned headdress'.*

The Death of Robin Hood

There were many Wakefield connections with **Kirklees Priory**; **William, 6th Earl de Warenne** was one of the founders, **Elizabeth de Staynton** of Woolley was prioress in Robin's lifetime and Robin's neighbour on Bichil, **Thomas Alayn,** retired there as a pensioner. The ballads say that, after 22 years as an outlaw (in **1347?**), Robin, with Little John, came here for bloodletting, then a common treatment for inflammation. We know that the nuns of Kirklees practised bloodletting, despite a prohibition. **Sir Roger of Doncaster**, an old enemy of Robin's, is said to have plotted with the prioress in his death. Little John helped Robin shoot one last arrow from the upper room in the priory gatehouse. Legend has it that he was buried where the arrow fell to earth. As the word 'Thom[as]' appears on the original gravestone (now lost), his neighbour Thomas Alayn may have been buried with him.

Three Nuns. *Walk the Kirklees Way (2002)*, Nigel Patrick & Peter Williamson, *p.31*. **3.** *The Origins of Robin Hood (2004)*, David Greenwood, *p.14*. **Robin's death:** *A Grave Tale*, David Hepworth, *p.112*, in *Robin Hood, Medieval and Post-Medieval*, Ed. Helen Phillips (2005). **Gatehouse etching** ; *The True History of Robin Hood*, J.W.Walker.

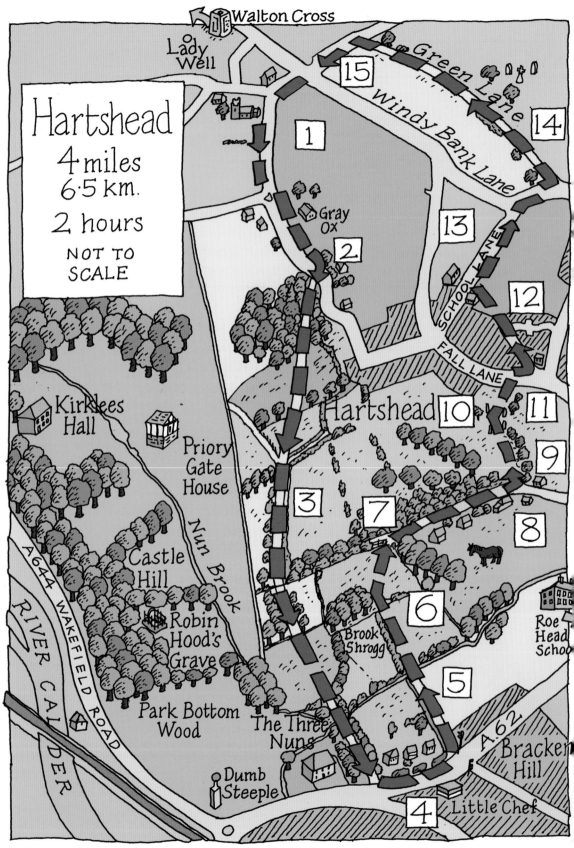

Walton Cross

Lady Well

Hartshead
4 miles
6.5 km.
2 hours
NOT TO SCALE

Green Lane

Windy Bank Lane

15

1

Gray Ox

2

School Lane

13

12

Fall Lane

Kirklees Hall

Priory Gate House

Nun Brook

Hartshead

10

11

9

3

7

8

Castle Hill

Robin Hood's Grave

Brook Shrogg

6

Roe Head School

A644 WAKEFIELD ROAD

RIVER CALDER

Park Bottom Wood

The Three Nuns

5

A62

Bracken Hill

Dumb Steeple

4

Little Chef

Hartshead

Parking: Church Lane opposite Hartshead Church (but please note there are services on Sunday mornings)
Buses: 225, 256 and 229 (Hartshead village) **OS ref**. SE 179 233

1. With the church on your right, walk southwards down **Church Lane**, and in quarter of a mile at the bend turn left down **Hartshead Lane**.

2. Pass **The Gray Ox** and after the left-hand bend take the footpath on your right. Follow the path through woodland, crossing a railway sleeper bridge over a ditch then go straight across the field ahead. Passing through a narrow hedge of trees into the next field the path goes down at 45° to the bottom right corner. *Look for **Kirklees Hall** and **Castle Hill**, site of Robin Hood's grave, across the valley to your right.*

3. Take the track ahead, part of the **Kirklees Way**. At the end of the track cross the stile by the metal gate and go ahead across the field to cross another stile. A track brings you out at the side of the **Three Nuns** public house.

4. Turn left alongside the A62 and in 300 yards, just before you reach a set of traffic lights, take the footpath to your left between hedges.

5. The path skirts around the edge of a garden then emerges at a railway sleeper bridge over a small stream. Continue up the left side of the field ahead.

6. A stile takes you along the right-hand end of **Brook Shrogg**. Continue ahead, over a second stile and onwards for another 30 yards then turn up the slope, diagonally across the field towards a stile in a wire fence at the left edge of the hilltop wood.

7. Turn right on the track and follow it for a quarter of a mile, ignoring the first footpath down into the hollow to your left and passing **Hartshead Hall Shire horse farm** and **Parkin Hall Stud** on your right.

8. When you reach a small group of cottages take the '**Public Footpath to Fall Lane**' down steps into the hollow on your left. Follow the sometimes nettly path onwards and to the right. The right of way appears to follow a sometimes impassable the holloway up the slope, beneath hollies and oaks, to emerge at the top with a broken wall on the right.

9. Turn right to pass between two stone gateposts with a hedge line of old thorn trees on your right. Pass through a second pair of gateposts then head towards a stile in the wall at the top of the slope.

10. Cross the road and walk up **Littlethorpe Hill** opposite.

11. When you reach the sharp bend turn left on the footpath by **Leah Cottage** and follow it across the playing fields.

12. Turn right up **School Lane** then, at the T-junction, right on **Windy Bank Lane** and in 100 yards turn left to follow **Green Lane**, a footpath across the fields for half a mile.

13. Turn left on **Hare Park Lane** and cross **Windy Bank Lane** at the crossroads to return to **Hartshead Church**.

Robin & the King

*"The Earl of Lancaster is that one,
And the Earl of Warenne sir John,
Bold and as hardy:
They mow do mycull with the king"*

King Edward and the Shepherd

IN THIS old ballad, in which **Adam the poacher** appears in the 'Robin Hood' role, **Lancaster** and **Warenne** exert their disproportionate (*mickle* or *muckle*) influence on the king with a sneer (*mow*). The conclusion of *A Little Gest of Robin Hood* appears to be set a year after the Battle of Boroughbridge when **Edward II** made a tour of the north, entering York on May Day and visiting Rothwell, May 16th to 21st, before moving on to Plumpton Park. He ended his tour in Nottingham where he stayed until the 24th November 1323.

In the *Gest* when the king hears that Robin has been taking deer in the forest, he disguises himself as an abbot and, deliberately walking into an ambush, meets the outlaw. Robin is pardoned and returns with the king to Nottingham and works for him for a year at court before returning to life in the greenwood. Court records reveal that in 1324 a **Robyn Hode** was employed as a valet.

| John de Faucomberg, Sheriff of Nottingham and Yorkshire fl. 1295-1330 | Thomas Plantagenet, 2nd Earl of Lancaster 1278-1322 | Isabella, She-wolf of France, Queen of England 1293-1358 | Edward of Caernarvon 1284-1327 King of England 1307-1327 | Hugh le Despenser Elder 1262-1326 Younger 1286-1326 | John 8th Earl de Warenne, lord of the manor of Wakefield 1286-1347 |

After Lancaster's death **John de Warenne** eventually regained the manor of Wakefield but he would be the last of his line. In 1331 'certain persons' *(Robin?!)* broke into his parks in Yorkshire and carried away 200 swans worth 100 marks and as many deer. **Joan de Barr**, Warenne's estranged wife, a companion of **Queen Isabella**, was with her when she died. **Hugh de Spencer** the younger was granted Wakefield parish church in 1325 but he was executed in 1327. Thomas's brother **Henry** became Earl of Lancaster and, in 1326, in league with **Isabella** and **Roger Mortimer**, captured the king. **Marlowe's** *Edward II* gives the **Bishop of Hereford** a role in the king's murder but in a letter of *c.*1337 one of the pope's secretaries in Avignon suggests that Edward escaped and lived for years as a hermit near Milan. I hope he did! In **Ben Jonson's** Robin Hood play *The Sad Shepherd* it seems that '**Reuben the Hermit**' is the king in disguise.

Pope John XXII 1249-1334